Margaret Angus
15 Markham Rd,
Wroughton
Swindon
  SN4 9JT.

TEL: 81302R

GW00717041

From: Tilda + Unc,
   6th August 1983.
   With lots of Love.

A NONSENSE BIRTHDAY BOOK

A NONSENSE BIRTHDAY BOOK

by Edward Lear

FREDERICK WARNE

Published by Frederick Warne (Publishers) Ltd, London 1980
Copyright © 1980 Frederick Warne (Publishers) Ltd

ISBN 0 7232 2406 4

Printed in Great Britain by
Butler & Tanner Ltd, Frome and London
D 6380·1180

PREFACE

Based on the first *Lear's Nonsense Birthday Book*, published in 1892 by Frederick Warne & Co. "in response to constant enquiries for a humorous Birthday Book", this redesigned version contains many Edward Lear illustrations and limericks chosen with care from his *Nonsense Omnibus*.

Although Lear is known as the Father of English Nonsense, he was careful to disclaim the credit of having created this type of rhyme, for he wrote in the preface to his book *More Nonsense*: "...the lines beginning, 'There was an old man of Tobago', were suggested to me by a valued friend, as a form of verse lending itself to limitless variety for Rhymes and Pictures; and thenceforth the greater part of the original drawings and verses for the first 'Book of Nonsense' were struck off with a pen, no assistance ever having been given to me in any way but that of uproarious delight and welcome at the appearance of every new absurdity".

There was an Old Derry down Derry,
Who loved to see little folks merry;
    So he made them a book,
      and with laughter they shook
At the fun of that Derry down Derry.

There was an Old Man with an owl,
Who continued to bother and howl;
    He sat on a rail
    And imbibed bitter ale,
Which refreshed that Old Man and his owl.

❆ January 1 ❆

Heather Angus (Cousin)

_____

_____

_____

❆ January 2 ❆

Gwen(doline) Morgans.

_____

_____

_____

❆ January 3 ❆

_____

_____

_____

_____

9

❄ January 4 ❄

❄ January 5 ❄

❄ January 6 ❄

There was a Young Lady of Sweden,
Who went by the slow train to Weedon;
    Why they cried, "Weedon Station!"
    She made no observation
But thought she should go back to Sweden.

There was a Young Lady of Welling,
Whose praise all the world was a-telling;
    She played on a harp,
    And caught several carp,
That accomplished Young Lady of Welling.

❈ January 7 ❈

❈ January 8 ❈

Elvis Aaron Presley

❈ January 9 ❈

❋ January 10 ❋

❋ January 11 ❋

❋ January 12 ❋

There was an Old Man who said, "Well!
Will *nobody* answer this bell?
    I have pulled day and night,
    Till my hair has grown white,
But nobody answers this bell!"

There was an Old Man of Aosta,
Who possessed a large cow, but he lost her;
  But they said, "Don't you see
  She has rushed up a tree?
You invidious Old Man of Aosta!"

❄ January 13 ❄

_____

_____

_____

_____

❄ January 14 ❄

_____

_____

_____

_____

❄ January 15 ❄

_____

_____

_____

_____

❋ January 16 ❋

❋ January 17 ❋

❋ January 18 ❋

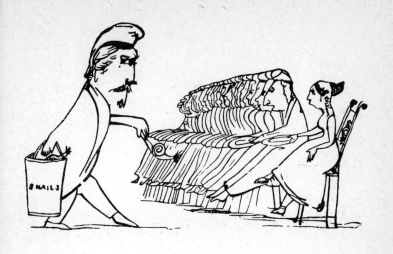

There was an Old Person of Sparta,
Who had twenty-five sons and one "darter";
    He fed them on snails,
    And weighed them in scales,
That wonderful Person of Sparta.

There was an Old Man of the West,
Who never could get any rest;
    So they set him to spin
    On his nose and his chin,
Which cured that Old Man of the West.

❈ January 19 ❈

_____

_____

_____

_____

❈ January 20 ❈

_____

_____

_____

_____

❈ January 21 ❈

_____

_____

_____

_____

❄ January 22 ❄

_____

_____

_____

_____

❄ January 23 ❄

_____

_____

_____

_____

❄ January 24 ❄

Celia Tonna _____

_____

_____

_____

There was an Old Man of the coast,
Who placidly sat on a post;
    But when it was cold
    He relinquished his hold
And called for some hot buttered toast.

There was an Old Man of the East,
Who gave all his children a feast;
But they all ate so much,
And their conduct was such
That it killed that Old Man of the East.

❄ January 25 ❄

_____

_____

_____

_____

❄ January 26 ❄

_____

_____

_____

_____

❄ January 27 ❄

_____

_____

_____

_____

❋ January 28 ❋

_____

_____

_____

_____

❋ January 29 ❋

_____

_____

_____

_____

❋ January 30 ❋

_____

_____

_____

_____

There was an Old Man in a Barge,
Whose Nose was exceedingly large;
    But in fishing by night,
    It supported a light,
Which helped that Old Man in a Barge.

There was an Old Person of Tring,
Who embellished his nose with a ring;
    He gazed at the moon
    Every evening in June,
That ecstatic Old Person of Tring.

Uncle Terry Gamble
Peter Day

~c~

※ February 2 ※

_____

_____

_____

_____

※ February 3 ※

_____

_____

_____

_____

※ February 4 ※

_____

_____

_____

_____

There was a Young Lady of Tyre,
Who swept the loud chords of a lyre;
    At the sound of each sweep
     She enraptured the deep,
And enchanted the city of Tyre.

There was a Young Lady of Troy,
Whom several large flies did annoy;
    Some she killed with a thump,
    Some she drowned at the pump,
And some she took with her to Troy.

❄ February 5 ❄

❄ February 6 ❄

❄ February 7 ❄

❉ February 8 ❉

_____

_____

_____

_____

❉ February 9 ❉

_____

_____

_____

_____

❉ February 10 ❉

_____

_____

_____

_____

There was an Old Person of Cheadle,
Who was put in the stocks by the beadle
    For stealing some pigs,
      Some coats, and some wigs,
That horrible Person of Cheadle.

There was an Old Person of Dutton,
Whose head was as small as a button,
    So, to make it look big,
    He purchased a wig,
And rapidly rushed about Dutton.

February 11

February 12

Emma Dyer.

February 13

❄ February 14 ❄

❄ February 15 ❄

Aunt Tuba's birthday

❄ February 16 ❄

There was an Old Man of Whitehaven,
Who danced a quadrille with a raven;
    But they said, "It's absurd
    To encourage this bird!"
So they smashed that Old Man of Whitehaven.

There was an Old Man of Coblenz,
The length of whose legs was immense;
 He went with one prance
 From Turkey to France,
That surprising Old Man of Coblenz.

❋ February 17 ❋

❋ February 18 ❋

Joanne Bodgers (Rodgers)

❋ February 19 ❋

❄ February 20 ❄

_____

_____

_____

_____

❄ February 21 ❄

_____

_____

_____

_____

❄ February 22 ❄

_____

_____

_____

_____

There was an Old Man who said, "How
Shall I flee from that horrible cow?
    I will sit on this stile,
    And continue to smile,
Which may soften the heart of that cow."

There was an Old Person of Rhodes,
Who strongly objected to toads;
    He paid several cousins
    To catch them by dozens,
That futile Old Person of Rhodes.

❉ February 23 ❉

_____

_____

_____

_____

❉ February 24 ❉

Cousin Timothy (1962)

_____

_____

_____

❉ February 25 ❉

Uncle Ray Green

_____

_____

_____

❄ February 26 ❄

❄ February 27 ❄

❄ February 28 ❄

There was a Young Person of Ayr,
Whose Head was remarkably square:
    On the top, in fine weather,
    She wore a Gold Feather,
Which dazzled the people of Ayr.

There was an Old Man whose despair
Induced him to purchase a Hare;
    Whereon one fine day,
    He rode wholly away,
Which partly assuaged his despair.

✳ February 29 ✳

◝◜

✳ March 1 ✳

❊ March 2 ❊

_____

_____

_____

_____

❊ March 3 ❊

_____

_____

_____

_____

❊ March 4 ❊

_____

_____

_____

_____

There was an Old Person of Troy,
Whose drink was warm brandy and soy,
Which he took with a spoon,
By the light of the moon,
In sight of the city of Troy.

There was an Old Man in a Marsh,
Whose manners were futile and harsh;
    He sate on a Log,
    And sang Songs to a Frog,
That instructive Old Man in a Marsh.

❋ March 5 ❋

❋ March 6 ❋

❋ March 7 ❋

❊ March 8 ❊

_____

_____

_____

_____

❊ March 9 ❊

_____

_____

_____

_____

❊ March 10 ❊

_____

_____

_____

_____

There was an Old Man of Leghorn,
The smallest that ever was born;
    But quickly snapped up he
    Was once by a puppy,
Who devoured that Old Man of Leghorn.

There was an Old Person of Chester,
Whom several small children did pester;
    They threw some large stones,
    Which broke most of his bones,
And displeased that Old Person of Chester.

❖ March 11 ❖

❖ March 12 ❖

❖ March 13 ❖

❧ March 14 ❧

❧ March 15 ❧

❧ March 16 ❧

There was an Old Man in a pew,
Whose waistcoat was spotted with blue;
    But he tore it in pieces
    To give to his nieces,
That cheerful Old Man in a pew.

There was an Old Man of the Wrekin,
Whose shoes made a horrible creaking;
    But they said, "Tell us whether
    Your shoes are of leather,
Or of what, you Old Man of the Wrekin?"

❄ March 17 ❄

❄ March 18 ❄

Uncle Alex's birthday
James Green   (1977)

❄ March 19 ❄

❄ March 20 ❄

_____

_____

_____

_____

❄ March 21 ❄

_____

_____

_____

_____

❄ March 22 ❄

Mary Day _____

_____

_____

_____

There was an Old Man who said, "Hush!
I perceive a young bird in this bush!"
 When they said, "Is it small?"
 He replied, "Not at all!
It is four times as big as the bush!"

There was an Old Lady of Prague,
Whose language was horribly vague;
 When they said, "Are these caps?"
 She answered, "Perhaps!"
That oracular Lady of Prague.

❊ March 23 ❊

_____

_____

_____

_____

❊ March 24 ❊

Robert Gamble (1971)

_____

_____

_____

❊ March 25 ❊

_____

_____

_____

_____

❋ March 26 ❋

~~Dad's birthday~~ See May 26th

❋ March 27 ❋

❋ March 28 ❋

There was an Old Person of Ewell,
Who chiefly subsisted on gruel;
 But to make it more nice
 He inserted some mice,
Which refreshed that Old Person of Ewell.

There was an Old Man of Cape Horn,
Who wished he had never been born;
    So he sat on a chair,
    Till he died of despair,
That dolorous Man of Cape Horn.

❈ March 29 ❈

_____

_____

_____

_____

❈ March 30 ❈

_____

_____

_____

_____

❈ March 31 ❈

_____

_____

_____

_____

❋ April 1 ❋

❋ April 2 ❋

❋ April 3 ❋

There was an Old Man with a nose,
Who said, "If you choose to suppose
    That my nose is too long,
     You are certainly wrong!"
That remarkable man with a nose.

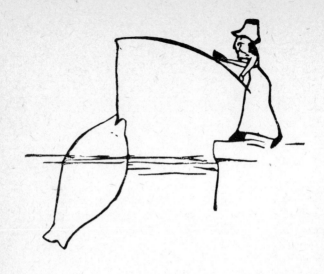

There was a Young Lady of Wales,
Who caught a large fish without scales;
    When she lifted her hook
    She exclaimed, "Only look!"
That ecstatic Young Lady of Wales.

❖ April 4 ❖

_____

_____

_____

_____

❖ April 5 ❖

_____

_____

_____

_____

❖ April 6 ❖

Auntie   Kathleen _____

_____

_____

_____

❋ April 7 ❋

❋ April 8 ❋

❋ April 9 ❋

There was an Old Man with a beard,
Who sat on a horse when he reared;
    But they said, "Never mind!
    You will fall off behind,
You propitious Old Man with a beard!"

There was an Old Person of Chili,
Whose conduct was painful and silly;
    He sat on the stairs
    Eating apples and pears,
That imprudent Old Person of Chili.

❄ April 10 ❄

Lisa Tonna (Best friend)

_____

_____

_____

❄ April 11 ❄

_____

_____

_____

_____

❄ April 12 ❄

_____

_____

_____

_____

❄ April 13 ❄

_____

_____

_____

_____

❄ April 14 ❄

_____

_____

_____

_____

❄ April 15 ❄

Auntie Carol

_____

_____

_____

There was an Old Person of Hurst,
Who drank when he was not athirst;
   When they said, "You'll grow fatter!"
   He answered, "What matter?"
That globular Person of Hurst.

There was a Young Lady of Portugal,
Whose ideas were excessively nautical;
    She climbed up a tree
    To examine the sea,
But declared she would never leave Portugal.

❈ April 16 ❈

_____

_____

_____

_____

❈ April 17 ❈

_____

_____

_____

_____

❈ April 18 ❈

_____

_____

_____

_____

❋ April 19 ❋

_____

_____

_____

_____

❋ April 20 ❋

_____

_____

_____

_____

❋ April 21 ❋

_____

_____

_____

_____

There was an Old Person of Gretna,
Who rushed down the crater of Etna;
    When they said, "Is it hot?"
    He replied, "No, it's not!"
That mendacious Old Person of Gretna.

There was an Old Man of Kilkenny,
Who never had more than a penny;
   He spent all that money
   In onions and honey,
That wayward Old Man of Kilkenny.

❋ April 22 ❋

_____

_____

_____

_____

❋ April 23 ❋

Sarer Beezer.

_____

_____

_____

❋ April 24 ❋

_____

_____

_____

_____

❋ April 25 ❋

Yvonne Tanna

❋ April 26 ❋

❋ April 27 ❋

There was an Old Person of Buda,
Whose conduct grew ruder and ruder,
    Till at last with a hammer
    They silenced his clamour,
By smashing that Person of Buda.

There was a Young Lady of Norway,
Who casually sat in a doorway;
  When the door squeezed her flat,
  She exclaimed, "What of that?"
This courageous Young Lady of Norway.

❄ April 28 ❄

_____

_____

_____

_____

❄ April 29 ❄

_____

_____

_____

_____

❄ April 30 ❄

_____

_____

_____

_____

❉ May 1 ❉

_____

_____

_____

_____

❉ May 2 ❉

_____

_____

_____

_____

❉ May 3 ❉

_____

_____

_____

_____

There was a Young Lady whose eyes
Were unique as to colour and size;
    When she opened them wide,
    People all turned aside,
And started away in surprise.

There was an Old Man of Quebec,—
A beetle ran over his neck;
    But he cried, "With a needle
    I'll slay you, O beadle!"
That angry Old Man of Quebec.

�֍ May 4 �֍

✷ May 5 ✷

✷ May 6 ✷

❋ May 7 ❋

❋ May 8 ❋

❋ May 9 ❋

There was an Old Man of Apulia,
Whose conduct was very peculiar;
    He fed twenty sons
    Upon nothing but buns,
That whimsical Man of Apulia.

There was an Old Man of Port Grigor,
Whose actions were noted for vigour;
    He stood on his head,
    Till his waistcoat turned red,
That eclectic Old Man of Port Grigor.

❋ May 10 ❋

❋ May 11 ❋

❋ May 12 ❋

Uncle Alec

❄ May 13 ❄

_____

_____

_____

_____

❄ May 14 ❄

_____

_____

_____

_____

❄ May 15 ❄

_____

_____

_____

_____

There was an Old Lady of France,
Who taught little Ducklings to dance;
    When she said, "Tick-a-tack!"—
    They only said, "Quack!"
Which grieved that Old Lady of France.

There was an Old Person of Bray,
Who sang through the whole of the Day
    To his Ducks and his Pigs,
    Whom he fed upon Figs,
That valuable Person of Bray.

❊ May 16 ❊

Grannie Williams

❊ May 17 ❊

Mrs. Tyler

❊ May 18 ❊

❋ May 19 ❋

Louise Hunter.

❋ May 20 ❋

❋ May 21 ❋

There was an Old Person of Filey,
Of whom his acquaintance spoke highly;
    He danced perfectly well
    To the sound of a bell,
And delighted the people of Filey.

There was an Old Person of Jodd,
Whose ways were perplexing and odd;
    She purchased a Whistle,
    And sate on a Thistle,
And squeaked to the people of Jodd.

May 22

May 23

May 24

Mrs Moody (D.H)

❊ May 25 ❊

❊ May 26 ❊

Dad's Birthday

❊ May 27 ❊

There was an Old Person of Sheen,
Whose expression was calm and serene;
    He sate in the water,
    And drank bottled porter,
That placid Old Person of Sheen.

There was an Old Man of the Isles,
Whose face was pervaded with smiles;
    He sung "High dum diddle,"
    And played on the fiddle,
That amiable man of the Isles.

❈ May 28 ❈

_____

_____

_____

_____

❈ May 29 ❈

_____

_____

_____

_____

❈ May 30 ❈

_____

_____

_____

_____

Catharine Green (1973)

There was an Old Lady of Chertsey,
Who made a remarkable curtsey;
    She twirled round and round
    Till she sank underground,
Which distressed all the people of Chertsey.

There was an Old Man of the Hague,
Whose ideas were excessively vague;
    He built a balloon
    To examine the moon,
That deluded Old Man of the Hague.

There was a Young Lady of Ryde,
Whose shoe-strings were seldom untied.
   She purchased some clogs,
    And some small spotted dogs,
And frequently walked about Ryde.

❊ June 1 ❊

❊ June 2 ❊

❊ June 3 ❊

Nicola Burnett -

❖ June 4 ❖

❖ June 5 ❖

❖ June 6 ❖

There was an Old Person of Dean,
Who dined on one Pea and one Bean;
    For he said, "More than that
    Would make me too fat,"
That cautious Old Person of Dean.

There was an Old Person of Dover,
Who rushed through a field of blue clover;
    But some very large bees
    Stung his nose and his knees,
So he very soon went back to Dover.

❄ June 7 ❄

Alison   Bishop.
Prince Rodgers Nelson

❄ June 8 ❄

❄ June 9 ❄

Jayne Russell.

❉ June 10 ❉

June Gamble (1967)

❉ June 11 ❉

❉ June 12 ❉

There was an Old Man with a beard,
Who said, "It is just as I feared!—
    Two Owls and a Hen,
    Four Larks and a Wren,
Have all built their nests in my beard!"

There was an Old Person of Dundalk,
Who tried to teach Fishes to walk;
    When they tumbled down dead,
    He grew weary, and said,
"I had better go back to Dundalk!"

❋ June 13 ❋

❋ June 14 ❋

Julia Haze (1983

❋ June 15 ❋

Bampi   Williams

❄ June 16 ❄

❄ June 17 ❄

❄ June 18 ❄

Auntie Beryl (F. Godmother)

There was an Old Man of El Hums,
Who lived upon nothing but Crumbs,
    Which he picked off the ground,
    With the other birds round,
In the roads and the lanes of El Hums.

There was an Old Man of Vesuvius,
Who studied the words of Vitruvius;
    When the flames burnt his book,
    To drinking he took,
That Morbid Old Man of Vesuvius.

❄ June 19 ❄

_____

_____

_____

_____

❄ June 20 ❄

_____

_____

_____

_____

❄ June 21 ❄

_____

_____

_____

_____

June 22

June 23

June 24

Ludovic Chassin's birthda

There was a Young Lady of Lucca,
Whose lovers completely forsook her;
    She ran up a tree,
    And said, "Fiddle-de-dee!"
Which embarrassed the people of Lucca.

There was an Old Man of Nepaul,
From his horse had a terrible fall;
    But, though split quite in two,
    With some very strong glue
They mended that Man of Nepaul.

❋ June 25 ❋

❋ June 26 ❋

❋ June 27 ❋

James + Carolina Llewelyn
(1970)

There was an Old Person of Nice,
Whose associates were usually Geese.
    They walked out together,
    In all sorts of weather,
That affable Person of Nice!

There was an Old Person of Cassel,
Whose Nose finished off in a Tassel;
    But they call'd out, "Oh well!—
    Don't it look like a bell!"
Which perplexed that Old Person of Cassel.

❄ July 1 ❄

❄ July 2 ❄

❄ July 3 ❄

❋ July 4 ❋

❋ July 5 ❋

❋ July 6 ❋

Sarah stacey (1968)

There was a Young Person in Red,
Who carefully covered her Head,
  With a bonnet of leather,
  And three lines of feather,
Besides some long ribands of red.

There was an Old Man of Dunluce,
Who went out to sea on a Goose;
    When he'd gone out a mile,
    He observ'd with a smile,
"It is time to return to Dunluce."

❋ July 7 ❋

_____

_____

_____

_____

❋ July 8 ❋

_____

_____

_____

_____

❋ July 9 ❋

_____

_____

_____

_____

❉ July 10 ❉

❉ July 11 ❉

❉ July 12 ❉

There was an Old Man of the Dee,
Who was sadly annoyed by a flea;
    When he said, "I will scratch it,"
    They gave him a hatchet,
Which grieved that Old Man of the Dee.

There was a Young Person of Janina,
Whose uncle was always a-fanning her;
  When he fanned off her head,
  She smiled sweetly and said,
"You propitious Old Person of Janina!"

❋ July 13 ❋

❋ July 14 ❋

❋ July 15 ❋

❊ July 16 ❊

❊ July 17 ❊

❊ July 18 ❊

There was an Old Person of Shoreham,
Whose habits were marked by decorum;
    He bought an Umbrella,
    And sate in the cellar,
Which pleased all the people of Shoreham.

There was an Old Person of Mold,
Who shrank from sensations of cold;
    So he purchased some muffs,
    Some furs, and some fluffs,
And wrapped himself up from the cold.

❋ July 19 ❋

❋ July 20 ❋

❋ July 21 ❋

Auntie Janet (voice)

❈ July 22 ❈

_____

_____

_____

_____

❈ July 23 ❈

_____

_____

_____

_____

❈ July 24 ❈

Nanna White _____

_____

_____

_____

There was an Old Person of Philæ,
Whose conduct was dubious and wily;
    He rushed up a palm
    When the weather was calm,
And observed all the ruins of Philæ.

There was an Old Man of the North,
Who fell into a basin of broth;
    But a laudable cook
    Fished him out with a hook,
Which saved that Old Man of the North.

❋ July 25 ❋

_____

_____

_____

_____

❋ July 26 ❋

Auntie Carolynn.

_____

_____

_____

❋ July 27 ❋

_____

_____

_____

_____

❖ July 28 ❖

❖ July 29 ❖

Lauren Miller

❖ July 30 ❖

There was an Old Person of Ickley,
Who could not abide to ride quickly;
    He rode to Karnak
    On a Tortoise's back,
That moony Old Person of Ickley.

There was an Old Person of Putney,
Whose food was roast spiders and chutney,
    Which he took with his tea,
    Within sight of the sea,
That romantic Old Person of Putney.

❋ July 31 ❋

つく

❋ August 1 ❋

❋ August 2 ❋

❋ August 3 ❋

❋ August 4 ❋

There was an Old Person of Skye,
Who waltz'd with a Bluebottle Fly:
    They buzz'd a sweet tune,
    To the light of the moon,
And entranced all the people of Skye.

There was an Old Man of Boulak,
Who sate on a Crocodile's back;
　　But they said, "Tow'rds the night
　　He may probably bite,
Which might vex you, Old Man of Boulak!"

❈ August 5 ❈

_____

_____

_____

_____

❈ August 6 ❈

Panda, tinkle, Randolph +
Ruth's birthday.

_____

_____

❈ August 7 ❈

Giselle   Manse (Driselly

_____

_____

_____

❄ August 8 ❄

❄ August 9 ❄

❄ August 10 ❄

There was an Old Person of Brigg,
Who purchased no end of a Wig;
    So that only his Nose
    And the end of his Toes
Could be seen when he walked about Brigg.

There was an Old Person of Bromley,
Whose ways were not cheerful or comely;
    He sate in the dust,
     Eating Spiders and Crust,
That unpleasing Old Person of Bromley.

❊ August 11 ❊

_____

_____

_____

_____

❊ August 12 ❊

_____

_____

_____

_____

❊ August 13 ❊

_____

_____

_____

_____

❋ August 14 ❋

❋ August 15 ❋

❋ August 16 ❋

There was an Old Person of Bude,
Whose deportment was vicious and crude;
    He wore a large Ruff
    Of pale straw-coloured stuff,
Which perplexed all the people of Bude.

There was an Old Person of Shields,
Who frequented the valleys and fields;
    All the mice and the cats,
    And the snakes and the rats,
Followed after that Person of Shields.

❈ August 17 ❈

❈ August 18 ❈

❈ August 19 ❈

❋ August 20 ❋

_____

_____

_____

_____

❋ August 21 ❋

_____

_____

_____

_____

❋ August 22 ❋

_____

_____

_____

_____

There was an Old Person of Rimini,
Who said, "Gracious! Goodness! O Gimini!"
    When they said, "Please be still!"
    She ran down a Hill,
And was never more heard of at Rimini.

There was an Old Man of the West,
Who wore a pale plum-coloured vest;
    When they said, "Does it fit?"
    He replied, "Not a bit!"
That uneasy Old Man of the West.

❅ August 23 ❅

Mr. Wern (violin S.Y.M. conductor)

❅ August 24 ❅

❅ August 25 ❅

169

❊ August 26 ❊

Sara Preston (friend)

❊ August 27 ❊

❊ August 28 ❊

There was an Old Man who screamed out
Whenever they knocked him about;
    So they took off his boots,
    And fed him with fruits,
And continued to knock him about.

There was an Old Man at a Junction,
Whose feelings were wrung with compunction,
    When they said, "The train's gone!"
    He exclaimed, "How forlorn!"
But remained on the rails of the Junction.

❈ August 29 ❈

❈ August 30 ❈

❈ August 31 ❈

❋ September 1 ❋

❋ September 2 ❋

❋ September 3 ❋

Mum's Birthday

Sophie Powers

There was an Old Man of Peru,
Who watched his wife making a stew;
    But once by mistake,
    In a stove she did bake
That unfortunate Man of Peru.

There was an Old Man of Dunrose;
A Parrot seized hold of his Nose.
    When he grew melancholy,
      They said, "His name's Polly,"
Which soothed that Old Man of Dunrose.

❉ September 4 ❉

Rebeccah's birthday (R. ANGUS)

❉ September 5 ❉

Auntie Jill Green

❉ September 6 ❉

❉ September 7 ❉

_____

_____

_____

_____

❉ September 8 ❉

_____

_____

_____

_____

❉ September 9 ❉

christopher

Christopher Jephson

_____

_____

_____

There was a Young Lady of Dorking,
Who bought a large bonnet for walking;
    But its colour and size
    So bedazzled her eyes,
That she very soon went back to Dorking.

There was an Old Person of Slough,
Who danced at the end of a Bough;
  But they said, "If you sneeze,
  You might damage the trees,
You imprudent Old Person of Slough."

❋ September 10 ❋

❋ September 11 ❋

❋ September 12 ❋

Timmy Jephson

❄ September 13 ❄

_____

_____

_____

_____

❄ September 14 ❄

_____

_____

_____

_____

❄ September 15 ❄

_____

_____

_____

_____

There was an Old Person of Grange,
Whose manners were scroobious and strange;
    He sailed to St. Blubb,
    In a Waterproof Tub,
That aquatic Old Person of Grange.

There was an Old Person of Bar,
Who passed all her life in a Jar,
    Which she painted pea-green,
    To appear more serene,
That placid Old Person of Bar.

❈ September 16 ❈

❈ September 17 ❈

❈ September 18 ❈

❄ September 19 ❄

_____

_____

_____

_____

❄ September 20 ❄

_____

_____

_____

_____

❄ September 21 ❄

_____

_____

_____

_____

There was a Young Lady of Greenwich,
Whose garments were border'd with Spinach;
    But a large spotty Calf
    Bit her Shawl quite in half,
Which alarmed that Young Lady of Greenwich.

There was an Old Person of Ealing,
Who was wholly devoid of good feeling;
    He drove a small Gig,
    With three Owls and a Pig,
Which distressed all the People of Ealing.

❄ September 22 ❄

_____

_____

_____

_____

❄ September 23 ❄

Auntie Katherine

_____

_____

_____

❄ September 24 ❄

_____

_____

_____

_____

❄ September 25 ❄

❄ September 26 ❄

❄ September 27 ❄

There was an Old Person of Pinner,
As thin as a lath, if not thinner;
    They dressed him in white,
    And roll'd him up tight,
That elastic Old Person of Pinner.

There was an Old Person of Fife,
Who was greatly disgusted with life;
    They sang him a ballad,
    And fed him on Salad,
Which cured that Old Person of Fife.

❖ September 28 ❖

❖ September 29 ❖

❖ September 30 ❖

Auntie Ann (Miller)

❋ October 1 ❋

Auntie Janine

❋ October 2 ❋

❋ October 3 ❋

Robert's Birthday (R. ANG

There was a Young Person whose History
Was always considered a Mystery;
    She sate in a Ditch,
    Although no one knew which,
And composed a small treatise on History.

There was an Old Man of Dumbree,
Who taught little Owls to drink Tea;
    For he said, "To eat mice
    Is not proper or nice,"
That amiable Man of Dumbree.

❊ October 4 ❊

_____
_____
_____

_____

❊ October 5 ❊

Uncle____Peter_____
_____
_____

_____

❊ October 6 ❊

_____
_____
_____
_____

❖ October 7 ❖

❖ October 8 ❖

❖ October 9 ❖

There was an Old Man of the Border,
Who lived in the utmost disorder;
  He danced with the Cat,
  And made Tea in his Hat,
Which vexed all the folks on the Border.

There was an Old Lady whose folly
Induced her to sit in a holly;
  Whereupon, by a thorn
  Her dress being torn,
She quickly became melancholy.

❊ October 10 ❊

❊ October 11 ❊

Caroline Hale. (Best friend)

❊ October 12 ❊

❄ October 13 ❄

❄ October 14 ❄

❄ October 15 ❄

There was an Old Man of Dee-side,
Whose Hat was exceedingly wide;
    But he said, "Do not fail,
    If it happen to hail,
To come under my Hat at Dee-side!"

There was an Old Person of Hyde,
Who walked by the shore with his Bride,
    Till a Crab who came near,
    Fill'd their bosoms with fear,
And they said, "Would we'd never left Hyde!"

❖ October 16 ❖

❖ October 17 ❖

❖ October 18 ❖

❧ October 19 ❧

❧ October 20 ❧

❧ October 21 ❧

There was an Old Person of Cromer,
Who stood on one leg to read Homer;
    When he found he grew stiff,
    He jumped over the cliff,
Which concluded that Person of Cromer.

There was an Old Man of Ancona,
Who found a small Dog with no Owner,
    Which he took up and down
    All the streets of the town;
That anxious Old Man of Ancona.

❋ October 22 ❋

_____

_____

_____

_____

❋ October 23 ❋

_____

_____

_____

_____

❋ October 24 ❋

_____

_____

_____

_____

❈ October 25 ❈

❈ October 26 ❈

❈ October 27 ❈

There was an Old Person in Gray,
Whose feelings were tinged with dismay;
　　She purchased two Parrots
　　And fed them with Carrots,
Which pleased that Old Person in Gray.

There was an Old Man of West Dumpet,
Who possessed a large Nose like a Trumpet;
　　When he blew it aloud,
　　It astonished the crowd,
And was heard through the whole of West Dumpet.

❈ October 28 ❈

Auntie Shirley

❈ October 29 ❈

❈ October 30 ❈

❋ October 31 ❋

_____

_____

_____

_____

_____

_____

❀

❋ November 1 ❋

_____

_____

_____

_____

_____

_____

There was an Old Man, who when little
Fell casually into a Kettle;
    But, growing too stout,
    He could never get out,
So he passed all his life in that Kettle.

There was a Young Lady whose nose
Was so long that it reached to her toes;
   So she hired an old lady,
    Whose conduct was steady,
To carry that wonderful nose.

❋ November 2 ❋

Uncle Chris (King)

❋ November 3 ❋

❋ November 4 ❋

❈ November 5 ❈

_____

_____

_____

_____

❈ November 6 ❈

My birthday_____

_____

_____

_____

❈ November 7 ❈

_____

_____

_____

_____

There was an Old Man of Dunblane,
Who greatly resembled a Crane;
     But they said,—"Is it wrong,
     Since your legs are so long,
To request you won't stay in Dunblane?"

There was an Old Person of Pett,
Who was partly consumed by regret;
    He sate in a cart,
    And ate cold Apple Tart,
Which relieved that Old Person of Pett.

❈ November 8 ❈

Nikki Jephson (Yuech)
Elaneor Haze.

❈ November 9 ❈

❈ November 10 ❈

❊ November 11 ❊

❊ November 12 ❊

❊ November 13 ❊

There was an Old Person of Brill,
Who purchased a Shirt with a Frill;
    But they said, "Don't you wish
    You mayn't look like a fish,
You obsequious Old Person of Brill?"

There was a Young Lady of Bute,
Who played on a silver-gilt flute;
   She played several jigs
    To her uncle's white pigs,
That amusing Young Lady of Bute.

❄ November 14 ❄

_____

_____

_____

_____

❄ November 15 ❄

Vanessa Crossley (1976)

_____

_____

_____

❄ November 16 ❄

_____

_____

_____

_____

❄ November 17 ❄

❄ November 18 ❄

❄ November 19 ❄

There was an Old Man of Thames Ditton,
Who called out for something to sit on:
    But they brought him a Hat,
    And said, "Sit upon that,
You abruptious Old Man of Thames Ditton!"

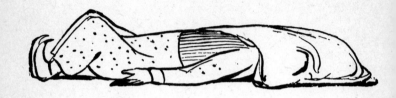

There was an Old Man of Hong Kong,
Who never did anything wrong;
    He lay on his back,
     With his head in a sack,
That innocuous Old Man of Hong Kong.

❊ November 20 ❊

- -

- -

- -

- -

❊ November 21 ❊

- -

- -

- -

- -

❊ November 22 ❊

Bindy (Belinda Sparrow)

- -

- -

- -

❧ November 23 ❧

_____

_____

_____

_____

❧ November 24 ❧

_____

_____

_____

_____

❧ November 25 ❧

_____

_____

_____

_____

There was an Old Person of Cannes,
Who purchased three Fowls and a Fan;
　　Those she placed on a Stool,
　　And to make them feel cool
She constantly fanned them at Cannes.

There was a Young Lady whose chin
Resembled the point of a pin;
    So she had it made sharp,
    And purchased a harp,
And played several tunes with her chin.

❖ November 26 ❖

Madeline King
Elaine Hawkins

❖ November 27 ❖

❖ November 28 ❖

❄ November 29 ❄

_____

_____

_____

_____

_____

_____

_____

❄ November 30 ❄

_____

_____

_____

_____

_____

_____

_____

There was an Old Man of Messina,
Whose daughter was named Opsibeena;
　　She wore a small Wig,
　　And rode out on a Pig,
To the perfect delight of Messina.

There was an Old Man on whose nose,
Most birds of the air could repose;
    But they all flew away
    At the closing of day,
Which relieved that Old Man and his nose.

✳ December 1 ✳

✳ December 2 ✳

✳ December 3 ✳

❄ December 4 ❄

❄ December 5 ❄

Joanne Moore

❄ December 6 ❄

There was an Old Man of Calcutta,
Who perpetually ate bread and butter,
    Till a great bit of muffin,
    On which he was stuffing,
Choked that horrid Old Man of Calcutta.

There was an Old Person of Wilts,
Who constantly walked upon Stilts;
    He wreathed them with lilies
    And daffy-down-dillies,
That elegant Person of Wilts.

❊ December 7 ❊

❊ December 8 ❊

❊ December 9 ❊

❉ December 10 ❉

❉ December 11 ❉

Auntie Olive

❉ December 12 ❉

There was an Old Person in Black,
A Grasshopper jumped on his back;
When it chirped in his ear,
He was smitten with fear,
That helpless Old Person in Black.

There was an Old Person of Ems,
Who casually fell in the Thames;
    And when he was found
    They said he was drowned,
That unlucky Old Person of Ems.

❋ December 13 ❋

Adrian King (1969)

❋ December 14 ❋

❋ December 15 ❋

❄ December 16 ❄

_____

_____

_____

_____

❄ December 17 ❄

Tommy Steel

_____

_____

_____

❄ December 18 ❄

Barney (Barnaby Paxes)

_____

_____

_____

There was an Old Person of Rye,
Who went up to town on a Fly;
    But they said, "If you cough,
    You are safe to fall off!
You abstemious Old Person of Rye!"

There was an Old Person of Ware,
Who rode on the back of a Bear;
    When they ask'd, "Does it trot?"—
    He said, "Certainly not!
He's a Moppsikon Floppsikon Bear!"

❄ December 19 ❄

_____

_____

_____

_____

❄ December 20 ❄

_____

_____

_____

_____

❄ December 21 ❄

_____

_____

_____

_____

❄ December 22 ❄

❄ December 23 ❄

❄ December 24 ❄

There was an old Person of Crowle,
Who lived in the Nest of an Owl;
    When they screamed in the Nest,
    He screamed out with the rest,
That depressing Old Person of Crowle.

There was an Old Person of Bree,
Who frequented the depths of the Sea;
   She nurs'd the small fishes,
   And washed all the dishes,
And swam back again into Bree.

❈ December 25 ❈

_____

_____

_____

_____

❈ December 26 ❈

_____

_____

_____

_____

❈ December 27 ❈

_____

_____

_____

_____

❈ December 28 ❈

Auntie Phelis

❈ December 29 ❈

❈ December 30 ❈

254

There was an Old Person of Woking,
Whose mind was perverse and provoking;
    He sate on a rail,
    With his head in a Pail,
That illusive Old Person of Woking.

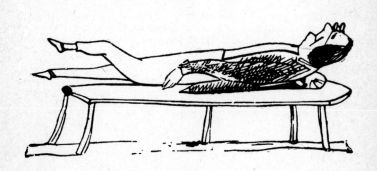

There was an old Man of Moldavia,
Who had the most curious behaviour;
  For while he was able
  He slept on a table,
That funny Old Man of Moldavia.